ON FATHERS < ON DAUGHTYRS

ON FATHERS < ON DAUGHTYRS
TIM ATKINS

BOILER HOUSE PRESS

There is a poetry in mere existence,
the kind that shopkeepers and people walking along the street lead,
you know, and evenness, that fills them up to whatever brim
is there, and stays, transient, all the days of their lives.
Such enharmonics are not for your poet-person. He sees, and breeds:
otherwise the game isn't worth the candle to him.
    — John Ashbery

My daughter, my daughter, what can I say
Of living?
    — George Oppen

The baby / sits in her chair / smiling / shining / / on good & / bad alike
What does she care / for the false republics of the world?
    — Anselm Hollo

Little daughters / in the middle of the night / why are you not / asleep again?
The stomping ground / must always die down / and be / curtained away
But we don't mind / being looked at / we like it!
We lie awake / for hours / with happiness actually
    — Steve Malmude

I did what I wanted. And I brought two children into this world.
I respected the mystery and mastered nothing.
    — John Thorpe

children / dance to static / in the kitchen / the idea / is suffused with light
   — Tom Raworth

Maybe rebirth is simply HAVING KIDS
   — Jack Kerouac

Come father, come at the daughter's call
   — Walt Whitman

Where did my dottr go?
   — bill bissett

*Oh let me just flop down flat on the road like a big fat
jelly out of a bowl and never move again!*
   — Samuel Beckett

Baby sleeping / woman turning / man on fire
   — Bill Berkson

*it is a poem
but is it   the trewf? says the daughter
it is (he said*
   — Anselm Hollo

*To be a Papa is to speak as if one knew.
That it increases solitude, this too,
defines us.*
   — Michael Gizzi

Is the baby singing in you? yet.
   — Joseph Ceravolo

*Daddy
Daddy
A cricket sings*
   — Ko Un

I comb my daughter's hair.
Where are you going, stars?
  — Tomasz Salamun

The Poet is he who watches. And what does he see? Paradise.
  — Andre Gide

This Time We Are Both
  — Clark Coolidge

The clear music
'Come ye daughters, share my anguish—'
  — Louis Zukofsky

The right place for a thing is where you find it.
  — Jimmy Schuyler

The long days,

    Rose

Setting out or staying at home

    Here we am, apparent on the carpet

Natto glue Porky & some letters from Gert

                  Walt lost & wandering

In the beige weave, I-self, as the days. Say—

    I yam—on my knees

Here is a tonne-weight of tantrum

     Sand in the daughter &

Pound the daddy

  My flowers ate

   The Daisy & the Lily

In translation, named

  The Japanese stringed instrument similar to a zither & the

     Hope & the snow. Why do no men come to

 This particular poetry

   Mountain that is a pile-up of daughters?

I caught moss

  On the tops of my books, Dr Seuss, & scraped it off

At the back, this is my song of Thing 2 &

        Thing 1

    We go into the air with complaints or without

      Socks   no ideas but in

  We give attention to spiders & the snail hospital

   We are allowed to say we only here

We are we because we rule each other's heads faces & necks

     Controlling the amount of sun which pierces us

Engaged with the process of increasing the alphabet

 Of understanding what makes the revolution

  Double-jointed

It is

Being clean

It concerns love for

Insomnia, you have made me this,

Japanese, lapsarian, a woman, a thumb, a back on a

Little man

Made of play-doh with one blue eyeball and a red arm, an

ovary

With which to write books

Log of the equivalent love

Which I have left to cassettes

Wearing

For Miles, Peter, Rob, Mark, Laird, Gabe, Daniel, Thomas,

& Jeff

We all fathers of girls, girls!

How wonderful it is to write of

Friendship & fatherhood, the

Pleasures of YES!

Peace instead of

The gladiatorial punt

In the bullshit & the runch

        In South London all the babies I am

  An orienteering course without compass for the little legs

 Coming off in the small of the back near Box Hill

Only Joe Ceravolo could have known it he says

        If someone has your nature

& he adds

        Come to me under me / Venus is not

    Second in the gloss

  Daddy coffee my hand

Is of destroyed gold & who says

Plastic lasts forever when

All the gas has gone out of last year's red slide on the deck

Would you like

A bite of my mountain

Cheating at Jurassic Park

         Crazy golf

  On my 50th birthday in Colliers Wood & the shakes

Look this is Dracula's sock

There is no snow

Jacket without arms in   impossible

Chalk insects on the wall VERY scary

Enough to scrape off & hide in

I mean the powder

Thing 1 enters the tent with a stamp on my nuts

Thus prolonging the eclipse

In this poem I shall call you

Dinosaur barnacle button bon-bon grip joy

fancy trial K-kanga we juicy snow coats

The experiment remains one of searching

The creation of poetry runs parallel with the actual living of

life

Aiming to reduce body odour

In both

Upside down at the top of the London Eye

What flies through the air & wobbles?

At which the finger becomes no more

Skulls in the pound shop then

George Tysh—*Shop*/*Posh*, plus

Fox licks stump

       Daddy! Teddy's stopped

Breathing   So have I

Cowboys running over our legs

    What's the magic word, Yuki?

Mummy? Money?

You little—Jellycopter!

Thus!

 Does its exclusion lead to a reduction of levels of eczema

   & where can I get one

             I asked her

To put her hands on my body but I can't

      She said they're behind my head

Leaving home to live with a cactus

   4 days without snow   having a bowel movement

   meditation

  We all scream for ass cream

 Then this

Coming out party

        As if it were a magical cocoon

In which to burn croissants

    Because if you don't write it

  Do iPods get heavy when you fill them with music?

Daddy

     She begs me to stop singing

 The brown thing sinking into the centre of the lake

The two-fingered accordionist

I am a story times 5

How many sports involve feathers

Swimming with magic fish

      This as a line break

     At half term we attend the typical girls'

  suffragettes singers' workshop

   Caterpillars sent out

  To devour the government

The mouth of the green one is called the mandybile

It takes tiny bites out of 19 cookies & cakes

At each birthday

Belly Filmus, Doras, Hogan Gophers, Moon Swamp & Aprils

Moving her butt which she has not yet got

7 stickers for not whining

Breaking an egg by throwing it

Thing 1 becomes an angel when Thing 2 vomits into her

mouth

Covered in glo-stars

Shimmering gaily

When we jump we go pop

Dropping spiders in the butter to freak out the mother

Sleeping with a pumpkin

No theories about the quotidian, just the quotidian

Santas in the mall call

Attention to insects

Ejected from the Camden Arts Centre for having too good

a time

But that painting needed more green in it

Waiting at the kerb till the worms pass

An anxiety attack in the basement of City Lights

But it doesn't have one!

My face on a sunflower at the top of the totem pole

On the tip of John Betjeman's rocket

Jock the chimp / with an extra limp / deedle, deedle, deedle,

dum

Silent before 8 every morning

Stoned with Daniel at the moment of my father's death

Both girls on my back

Lovely!

Looking deep into Worcestershire for the last time

The goodness of cousins

We all seeing some

Light moving through space

Poetry being a ripple

You get double for a food word

Splashing in the cold brown sea of the Thames

Estuary

Don't get sick in the land of the asset stripped

We did

Growing something on the bone

Grazing on cupcake tops

Pure mathematics, bats, twats

Asleep in my sleeves

All people be happy   My starfish!

A huge head with arms legs & a mess

A shadow of ice exchanges the color of light

Driving & crying, Nusrat Fateh Ali Khan, Tooting

Refusing food, water, shocks

Selling teeth to the tooth fairy

One hundred per cent profit

Bouncing on everything till it breaks

Lying down to protest.

There will be no revolution

In the Penguin Book of Japanese Verse

Until all the babies have been changed

I am a Canadian artist

In an iron dog's pants

But the objective remains—to make sense of all

this

Why do no men come

Broke, heady, & speechless

Remembering Kerouac abandoned his daughter

I focus on family errands

& despise him for that

Washing the milk

Comedy is a man in trouble

Teaching tent etiquette

Daddy why's that

A blackbird dressed as a squirrel

Giving up when you get to the middle of a long word

The book that you toss was not boss

It was Dr Seuss   I am cross   & your punishment is

this

The emergence of the human family

Cutting your nails without shaking

Looking down at my little body in the white botanica

A man made of nux vomica milk shakes

    But not yet

I wrote that   Koto wrote this

  In the Batcave

    Past the Horned Gates

               Is this what you get for unrequited love

No escape from the great cycle of being

    A hooped marsupial

    Uxuriousness, osteomyelitis, a Dutch wife

               Que cono, tio!

  Uncle! What a cone!

Don't touch the volcano

        It's Halloween—& you cannot be Santa

Face down in the snow

    Political poetry in the academy

      Koalas in balaclavas

      Doing origami

  Cop this!

Not thinking not thinking   Thinking

Our job is to let go of anger & love everyone

Atkins, daughters, & chips

Reaching through the slats of the pier end at Brighton

For this is a Buddha realm of infinite beauty

Simple filial & desirable

Hotter than a duck's head

Face down in the scrambled eggs

My lungs fags & pinholes. Our communism—

A pea green boat

In great confusion & the moon

Makes it better, crying on the leg, staggered by

A stranger's freckled breast

The problem is not how to keep hold of it but the

opposite

The green man & the march of the bungalows

A Bronx cheer & the ink cigarette

All the things a daughter has to do

Constantly filled with bourgeois astonishment

I cannot stop it

The itch of the golden nit, well mildly, to a baby

The flambeau between my ribs & hips

I have a book. It's grown from spots

Hard not to look busy from behind

Holding the corn cob—with no front teeth to eat it

Lists serving to address we the sleepless

Taking the invisible splinter out of your foot

Beard turning grey

Using the chin to tickle

Green banana hurled at the wall

Bee-clouds at the eyebrows

Doing knee drops

Existing, wiped—

Giving a speech now

Talking to you like you're a baby

Looking older round the ears

Don't pretend you don't love me

Drinking glo-stick juice

These beans floating in space

Banned from YouTube

Prove we fucked at least once

　　All the puddles in the city to be jumped in, jumped in

　　　　Daddy, do planes go to the toilet?

What do you call a woman with a radiator on her head?

　　Hung in a bucket over the bend of the Thames, Anita

1. A man in a brown paper suit

(Russell)

2. Where the wild things ain't

　　As an experience of empathy & equality

　　We lost the moon

A gay dinosaur called

　　　No production, only interdependence

　　Run over in verbal reasoning

Rust round the rim of the brake

　　　Demonstrating, horse chestnut, Emily's

Elena, hello, cloud, back

　　On the picket line

　　Every snowflake falls in its place

For what—not against

  A language to come

                Without government mark or stamp

  Made the girl-fish turn human

      Deprived of linguistic vibrations

    Giving Ariana the chop, Sharlene one in the mouth

Going there on Google Earth

      Good enough

Sitting linked with non-profit

            a.k.a. Naomi, a.k.a. Kitty

Because / nobody knows me / like my / barnacle

  Face down in the cake

The way that love is, at dusk

      "Hidden from human knowledge or understanding"

        Rock would land on & saying

"If you send for a doctor, I <u>will</u> see him now"

        The world has gone to answer

In my heart, it is

A sponge of blue

I have feathers & she

Is snowing

    In the doorway

  Without soup

This earth & this

   Question

What are weaklings?

   Bones Festes lights strung down the Nou de la Rambla

The kitchen, strange, logically punk

      Beneath the plane trees, their beak falling

Bright molar

To be human for an instant

& then washing

   The floating world like a dish

  Where my arm goes to sleep

  That feeling of unending

 Love comes in, Thomas

Where the halogens roam

  Where the smell of uranium adds fruitcake to the

exchequer

Asleep on the beatnik

Cold air in my pants

Because milk starts out as grass

Perfect as they are

Perfect as they aren't

& so I

Tread on dandelions

Fall to thinking

Feel sorry that

Give up

Come to think

On all sides, I hear

The sounds of disaster

Free & red in your star

The bad poems   still bad

Dear love and all the faint world it reaches to, it wants

A palpitation like an envelope forecasting doom

Hiragana 'ice cream' or Katakana, the same

Centrifugal nature also seems

Shining with tea

Kissed in the cars

In the questionnaire about love

The Japanese stringed instrument similar to a zither & the

Hope & the snow

Biting your black hair for vitamins

Boom, boom, boom, wherever you are

The wind has blown my socks off

Mu is Um backwards

Baby nails

Black specks on the sheet

Down on the farm

The world is a very fucking place

Duck bark

Denby & the randy animals

Drop & drag

This marriage

Hiding the boot inside the boot

The same as the last

 Finding it

   In the syrupy and shimmering element

Losing it

     Too to two

    Small girls

Sailing through the night

   Wired to paternal circuits

Snored back to life

   & I have a small dreamy part

      Princesses in the family republic

   With one talent, jumping

  The father

Abandoned

     One shooting star, then another

  When the bits get stuck

A cream to cure ringworm

     I cannot reach with my teeth

  A whale & a triangle, you

Our small orchestra

You have my hair!

For attachment

Man on fire, woman sleeping

As the bones grow less dense

Crayons lose their taste

6 minutes for the light of the sun to reach the earth

10 minutes to drive from Tooting Broadway to Tooting

Bec

Kissing your cerebral cortex

The lord & owner of nobody's face

Say we will die, perhaps

Brushing sand from our cracks

Protesting—inside or outside the fence

(a) Fireman

On sleeping woman

Bookish, feverish

Under one day of sun

The whole summer long

The Poets of the Late T'ang

Looking at the carrots, watching

Go West Young Scoob

Clangers

Touching the firmament

On Bear's Head

Don't blow bubbles in your drink

In a world of damp planks

Had I only known

Holding sparklers on the stoop

My longing would be so great

Concerning the beauty of readymades

What's your favourite

Everything

Taking care to enunciate

For poets, for parents

Flashing down the spillway

Faster than thought

Sleeping in a cave

To avoid the bad mothers

Gas

 Sentences my daughter

 Face down in the alphabet app

Going to the Turner show at the Tate, she said,

     Tina or Ike?

I ran away to join the circus

(the flea circus)

  In search of the miraculous, love

                    My heart's the same

As an upturned flame

                  Rubbing at Apollinaire's grave

  Taking tea at the P.T.A.

     Teaching you to how to burp, we

Read *Visions of Cody*

Cutting the gum out

        Ears pop when the plane drops

        Poop in a Poundstretcher bag—plop!

   Taking a screwdriver to the verruca

Pictures of children

Starving

Gangnam style

Face down at the demo

The book glows where the eye goes

There is no escape

Giving Teddy a short back & sides

This is for Alice & Bernadette

Moving the snowman closer to the fire

It's not how big your share is but how much you can

share

Comparing theories

Coolidge covered with spinach

Dolls melt in the vent

Fossils really older than you are

Your hand & mine in the photocopier

Book signing with an ink-stained bum

Where utopia = your feet

Mud mittens

From Buster

A Bike peel

Falling from a cloud

28th of the third 2001

Carrer Poeta Cabanyes

The name changed by Franco

From the revolutionary Catalan

To the Castilian poet, so

To which hour does she grow

The skin of a Buddha

Peaceful round corners

Trampoline fever

Spurs to the spare future

Neurons

To which attach

String theory to a daughter

20th December 2008

All our journeys

Yabba-dabba don't

Steered by the tongue

Made a baby what—from a bottle of rum

English silk shapes like quivering

Where the woman becomes

Human entries, at last

No better body than the world

I can tell of

All surface = all depths

Coughing for the underdog

Too crying for driving

Leaving Hammy hopeful & helpless in the home for homeless

hamsters

Pee in my Pussy Riot pantoum

Marginalised & knackered

More by accident than design

In favour of

Compassion compromise & conversation

Over opposition the vocabulary & valorisation of violence

But this too in its way is a protest

The men without kids

All appear the most pressed

                    We are—fellow poets—

At the arc of the test

Dancing from the wrists & the ankles

In love nevertheless

                    Boring on fathers, on daughters

The great appear great

        Because we are on our knees

    It says here

Let us rise

        Out of droplets

    Midwinter Day

    First Baby Poems

        The Long Days, Rose

            Mutability

    Birds and Fancies

        Body Clock

                Songs for The Unborn Second Baby

Amedellin Nosegay Cooperative

I am leaving the house NOW

What happens when nothing happens

The birds in the sad

Park trees

& you cannot eat sticks

Attempting the same

On fathers, on daughters

The comma is optional

Allowing for lies and exaggeration

I cannot go anywhere because this is

The Ayatollah of London SW19

You want to go outside & look at the ice

We in 3 pairs of pants

Shining on futurism

The sun turned on albeit briefly

Seven small legs

Painting not on

But with the face

Cleaning the walls like the mind in the middle of the night

Always happy at the first sprint through it

The poem

Fighting sleep to meditate

Then film painting the cake

No fathers

With nothing to fear but to mothers

Alternately lazy or lubbing

In bed reading Roland, writing repeatedly

What did the food say, though

Upon the owner's C.V.

Is it blood, Normal?

Four Danish Gurus

Under Dining Room Gurus

For sale on ebay

Straight after the longest

The shortest day of the year

The self-righteousness of the ruler

A protest painted on cardboard

Love all or fuck it

Coming face to face with dense matter

Three fabulous roman candles

Totally ready to go

Centre of equal daughters

Popcorn in the haircut

Looking for the cat's face

Not writing for lego

Applying mouth-to-mouth resuscitation to a goldfish

Her helicopter hits   & falls burning from the top shelf

Hawkins Huidobro Hejinian

How do you make love to a mermaid?

Ask the 8 ball

It says

Waist in crashed chipmunk

Awake from the sugar rush

By reading Dogen

Training the baby

But who is not

Shouting to raise the temperature of a glass of

water

Reading 'Bob Dylan's

Irrational Fear of Foxes' by Een O'Reilly

Inhaling the smoke from the fireworks

A list of my Top 10 mistakes

The English weather

Banana splits, Pink Sabbath

Moustaches, glasses, sarongs

Legs go five ways

J.F.K.F.C.

Stopping at number 47

Reading Proust to a three-year-old

Would you rather be a triangle or a bee?

Face up at the ass doctor

Face down in Berlin

Stuck on page 3

Looking out the window, preparing for the test

The pears aren't the pears

The point at which Che picks up a gun

Filling the world with surprise

Toe of infinite power

Saying no to it

Mickeymauswitz, cheerios

Meddling

Beneath pylons

Kidzzz

Poems pile up

Using a microscope

Writing the vegetable record

Add your own meaning

A Kiss where your bone don't grow

Shadow at the end of the leg

On the picket line again

The Bob key is Frank

Resisting greed

The slap lollypop method

On the picket line again

A Bronx cheer for Dave & for Jez

Making star noises

Looking out across the Buddha fields

The Mayans get it right

Predicting the end of the welfare state

No longer on email

Grunting & screaming   instead

The revolutionary power of women's laughter

Leaving the courtroom

Concerning the content of utopias

Is it happiness?   Is it fulfilment?

Shall we

Overcome

Because I say so

The world is a very fucking place

Turning out to greet you

With no bangs   but love

Everybody pays the man with the cigar

So I got pregnant

Not wearing a hat   & after bite

Across the forehead   cut straight

Pop gone from the girls' bash

Blown back home

Over Battersea Bridge

To custard, political comics

The labour of mourning

Leaving Spain with an itch

Reading boyishly

Writing girlishly

We wet dream the revolution

Staying in education

Baking cakes

Holding on to young women

Not dropping them

Wrapping unwrapping repeatedly

Filming for when the eyes blown

Listening to *La Bamba*

At my funeral

Blowing balloons

On the picket line again

Face down at the wake

I'm girls, love, then

I'm men   making a man's salad, passive-aggressive

dressing

Amazed in the middle of cows

Late nights at the Tate

Plying the escalators

Making a career out of one good idea

In the shower with a sock monkey

Half asleep at the sleepover

One vegetable may hide another

At the table of correction

In the big book of germs

How to stay awake with a swan

Skin brushing

Saving sticks for the bonfire to send off the witch of Dulwich

With love (some) sparklers & a sausage

The hardest part's loving the bastards

Minus the apostrophe = the daddy pattern

As I was moving ahead

Right speech & blowing it

Concerning the greatness & awfulness of regional poets

Upon the long march

To a penthouse flat

In a Maoist cravat

Responsible for 80% of greenhouse gas

Us

Recycling lines from old poems

At Christmas on the Island of Women, swimming

Smoking a Gauloise underwater

& baby shit

Almost

Loving it

Staying up all night   On the lookout for Alzheimer's

Dreaming in the immensity of it all

Of   pamphlets   a few weeks in the sun

& once naked women

    Land   where the small press   chaps come most

  regularly

   Cleaning your milkteeth

Storing the old ones in boxes

Writing a new line every five minutes

   Fallen asleep on your spinach

We love the stars we haven't seen

We build a wall around the bad   oak leaves

  Am cabbage

Speaking homophonically

Before the arrival of boobs, menstrual blood

     No such thing yet

          Elsewhere   as heaven

Goofy & Pluto running government

   Having parties building cupcakes   over hospitals

  roads

          Good because they tell us

Liars

Aspiring to non-violence, this

A presence not absence

Sushi stuck to my glasses

Belly dancing the answer

Without centre, without affect, without narrative, only

children

On the carpet at the vortex

Sag aloo for breakfast

Your farts = Living Room Music

Searching for Ceremony Latin

Stepping in all the puddles in White City

& shouting

Fork'n knives to a waiter

Building a headache

Writing all day

To avoid the kids

Secretly fond of dirt

In your armpits

Life is passing   fast the blossom   covered donuts

The world's furious

Song fills our curtains

Make it New Malden

Salt coating the colon

cap on   not   *cat porn* off the leg

Poop covers *The Prelude*

As you twist

Reading it

To avoid having too good a morning

A's miscarriage

Tasting the water

J's miscarriage

Too small to draw

grapes

(not)   Laughing at baldies

Is what knowledge is

Human, wholly real

Your eye squished   My eye

In the mist

& not seeing

Beckton, Mount Fuji

Happy to get out of the tomato factory

                    Alive

            Without aim, without profit

The long days, Rose

            Katy's termination

        1987

        Repositions the peony

Free shoe with the Clark book

                    The punchline

Lemon entry

        My children, not owning them, my poetics

Impersonations of lettuce

Translating the dictionary

Matching the object to the ego

In a boat watching the steeple

Face down on the marble floors of the Gare du Nord

                Steak tartare

Never again

Pregnant

In every direction

Queuing up to leave the planet

Heart the place of a wren

Art the mark of two women

Not yet

In this life

Seeing everything

The aim of the poem is to live forever

With eye-drops that are the erasers of weasels

Where ignorant armpits clash by night

The aim of the poet is to live to eighty

With monstrous absorbency,

Total inclusion

& sleep once

Brave not to be brave

Watching it

Married to the void

& in ecstasy, & in error

This living

   What fukan theory

One big whack

      To Mr Potato Head

            Giving me tinnitus

Always gay   for three decades   meaning happy   parties

            Chewing heads off

                  The dinosaurs   candles

   Pass the food

Release the spirit

         Book   fondue

         Upon furious roundabouts

Baby sleeping, woman working, man not

            (Singing) trying, crying   playing spot the wig

         In Romford

Always moving towards   the pure land, something

            They call this one "a canapé?"

               & the lily, & the daisy

No ideas

But in kids   A poet is

A machine

Made out of girls

Life lived on hard drive

Skipping all the way to school

Bawling all the way back

This sky-filling land of South London

I am the one who rules it

Thing 2) You are a naughty genius

When you are tired, lie down

Alone in the universe

Because the universe is us

Not / *CHEESE!* / sandwiches

The wise will understand

Mountains make you sick

They're so pretentious

I'm glad I'm not Hitler

Needling the liver to heat up the kidney

Why don't they say I love you in Japanese

Because they don't

Getting hot

Over food porn & kittens

You write

'Like Cy Twombly'

Changing the sign to *Atkins & Father* from *Atkins & Daughters*

Boring & Fascinating

Bending double to sleep right

Mist & Dust

Yuk

Covers this English city

The debris, called otoconia, is called ear rocks

Mistranslating Cold Mountain

Having stolen my nerve endings

Thing 2 throws over some decibels

Butterflies = spiders with wings

Waking fish with a hammer to feed them

A small spot on Thing 1

Te quiero, the book says

Whether to leave it or squeeze it

Global warming caused by bad books

We begin by reducing your temperature

Always raining

Let me name them

Jesus!

A combination of Teletubbies & vigorous physical

activity

The desires of fathers to please   mothers in feathers

Tropes that grope at metaphysical significance

Sustaining wonder among moths

Trying to be attentive   failing

But isn't everything

Attention

Reading Bunny Lang

I want your dirt / upon my shirt

Burning aliens for earache

The any of

Blaming cereal

A burp's not an answer

Orange balls   floating in space

Igneous (Thing 1)

(Thing 2) Metamorphic

& the father

Sedentary, impossible, invisible

Drinking fossil fuel

Measuring everything

The car says

Hit the cushion & mean it

Reading fast in order to finish

High flip out in orbit mother

Baby gets carpet-burn on a patch five miles over Kazakhstan

Then the dogs catch the fox

Real snowstorm over London

The density (enlarging, gradually accumulating) of

time

Today in a bad mood everyone

Filming the capitalist edifice

      When we are dirt poor and we no longer have

mountains for shelter

  Joan of Arc, Wallace Stevens, soya beans

   & then you came when I thought it was impossible to

be happy

     In a different language

    Using joined-up writing if I don't want you to read it

       Philosophy based on the avoidance of pain

  Koto music   rhyming poems

No being

  le mot juste

       In a bear suit

          Without television

     Nothing touches this

        Magic corn age 11

Trying to fit the thermometer in

     Where Eadweard Muybridge died

At midnight

In search of penicillin

In a mall where stood / the great north wood

These lines from a dream

Two-fisted glitter pens

Squirting on something

Subhuti is overwhelmed by this teaching

Everywhere we look

Displaced persons

Wave the camera at the page

Dressed as a German, then

After-orgasm boredom, switching engines

I had nowhere to go in Walden

Asleep in the back seat in Kennington

Writing the poem to receive us

If abandoned language = this instant

I got a black no, two regular

An unknown three-hundred-and-twenty-nine-year-old Left-

Bank

intellectual

el Gusano Grande & the Chupacabra

Not just a high-spirited exercise in literary aggression

Sat on my lap

Typing this

Unable to stop

The pee leaking

Catalan Concrete poetry

Translation with a bucket of oxygen

In the poor corner of Barcelona's pleasure-quarter

The best part of the father, then

Drifts of daughters

Don't need religion to want to feed everyone

When the gerunds flood in

Clubbing each other   with telescopes

Where the night bends

The pencil   wonders

Or even a bit past it

Tooting in neon

Bird photos

Attain exemption from meaning

Concerning moss balls

Oh, honey, I—

Learnt this

Language from women

From men—competition, single syllables, irony, its

Efficacy, how not to love

animals, death by helicopter, abnegation

Passion, abandonment, writing off Popeye—

No wild gardens overlooked by night lights

Just sitting, aiming for nothing

In each genuine art work something appears that did not

exist before

For example

My darling

Wish for yous this—a good

Bullshit detector bra

Pa light stripped of sentiment

Resistance to dampness

The return of feminism for those who have left it

Good intention over gender

Strength at demonstrations & speed at fiestas

Self-worth & endurance

Knees that turn good

Regions, registers, people in all

Facility with organs

Skin to sun in leaping

Among the terrorist islands lawns willows sprinklers

Money gone to feed the rich

Some of them, some of it

Best to look at the blossom

If you close your eyes in this poem

Red of a stop sign

Stops everything / nothing we three caught in-between it

On our journey to the sun

High over South London Suburbs

In bunches in McDonalds

Privets in sparrows in Happy Meals cortinas

Identified by flipbook car parks horse chestnuts

Slowly dying

      Sign ahead   says sign   (sighing)

                        As it starts to increase

  Love—   All I can say with any certainty

             Punk rock's not that important

     Skidding down the road   with a donut

  Birds & dogs mesmerising trucks

        Thrush cream wiped over your bottom lip

Soundless as dots on a disc of snow

        Up the hill from the co-op

     Tinnitis now so loud that other people can hear it

 Converting thoughts into mp3s

Understanding, deleting

    The impulse of this poem is to leap outwards

     A little darker, more reclusive

You carrying your school bag

Me carrying you

    Daughter growing / father slowing

Every day

 Exactly the same

As the brick flies back in   right to left   panel   *ZIP!*

  Leaving the room to go to the moon

237 days to your birthday

                    Bored of everything, *Lil Angel*

The breath of taking, at 3AM   I have

      Occasionally   glimpsed   heaven

Awake in the economy of the uprising

                    What does the dove say   there at the window

 Often, love is hopeless

Drinking the roses

Craving for babies

    Conan picture on the wall

      Face down in the emotion

Poetry cursed by bad timing

            Flying to solid hollows

 At the leaves of grass party

Banging the plastic sax

Or the film of the snail

      Arrows bend to the school's back end

Life I love you less   in Januarys than   Aprils

  Hard to wake up with the damp in Joanne & less than

A quarter

   Of daylight on the head of each nail

     Pressing our faces to the little silver heads

Rays increasing

 Capacity for happiness

Bent towards it by attachment & sadness

           But what else is there beyond

Armies, insects, nectarines, economics,

      Alert on the shoe fields,

   Bulb after bulb. belly-to-belly

With Emily

      Face down in the

  Theatre or

   Rapture

     Night birds

Come to view the family

   Kicking books off the bed

     Making way for gas from another planet

Dragging the dead father

      Back into stanzas

  Two girls made   of armfuls   transistors

 Sailing gaps, baring fangs, chewing gum off the shoe

 bottom

Heart running up the stethoscope

   On the A23   Say leaving the sea

 Nurse burns of all possible peoples

  Wooden stars banged into things   chocolate chips

 sleeplessness with two kids

    & have & am—

  The road into Croydon   is bliss & this

     Lullaby is tuncless

With a surfeit of hotdogs

Bowling home   at 2AM   from Brighton   in dresses & sutras

  Stop   when you get to the end of these

Revolutionary Letters

              I am   Miss World   in search of you-

   know-what

      The alleviation of you-know-who

& world peace

       Of course

          I feel you on the phone

With the phone in your hand

Connected to the great chain of godfathers

                Pressing the daddy

To squeeze out the atom

      A little further

             Beyond the countryside, sporadically

I am nothing if I can't make you happy

           In bed with a panda

                 With quiet smells, pieces

           Three times pinched

     But never once sentenced

          Under the correct label

Your left paw   teaching me   Geography

c.f. The world, within   airports castles   & vice-versa

All the words waiting

This oscillation

When you're eleven

Every day

Different temperatures

In each leg

Because it is spring   & all & the dome   draws the girl

from the man

Deer here   in the park

Breathing in

Moons from your skin

Polymers   attached to lashes

With an apostrophe "s" headache

Dedicating this merit

To all sentient creatures

Including terrorists, tories, Tony   you'll see

When you love someone

It's easy

Pursuing a policy of non-violence   in Colliers Wood, at least

Let The Hip Gahn be

There for me

On dealing with bastards

(For—kids—there are many)

In this neck of the woods

The bigger the office, the bigger the ass

Which sits upon us

This against which   we have

Love & utopian   duffle-coats   bad hair   ukuleles

& the drift of good history   albeit slowly

The 99%   on the picket line again

Wet at the march   uncool & outraged

At the demo

Sign says NO CUTS

See it saying NO CUNTS

Stop

By the river

For an ice-cream

Filming things holding hands thanking jah for the whistles

    & banners

                     Yes & excited

          These the tasks

 In the land of two choices

Grow up scared or   (b)   Grow up scary

      Read an angry poem about it,   Tim

How pathetic

      Blowing our wages at the aquarium

        Sighing at fish

      Building kids out of chips

        Everything   beautiful   tasty

Moisturized for increased shine

  At Baudelaire's grave

 I am so snowed for you to sleep—

by Georgette

Rewriting life   to indicate love   At Vallejo's

        Moved to Montparnasse

From the communist cemetery in Montrouge

To orchestrate the freedom of lives,

To make them seem spacious and variable

Great on Super 8

After death   changing   things   extraordinary breakfasts

The names of lovers, own face   or forgetting   history

With no fixed point to love from

One can only love everything

Knew this once on the carpet

& in poems

Show it

Through an absence of poetics

All the new discoveries come

Inhaling pollution

To make the air cleaner

From outside the academy

Testing drones in the poem

Here we are   drawn by women

Naturalist abstract

Unfucked by entitlement or anxiety

Not holding the bottle but

Herewith

Thing 1 on my shoulders

In a shack in Vancouver

In the snow in my imagination in Tooting

Spooning noodles from a wooden bowl into the unhungry

daughter

Not filled with life but life

Itself escaping, tripping

& wrong-"*about*"-writing

Three million pieces in the old style

So I'll chew your food for you

Not remembered but

Filmed it

Is a life worth living

In Worcestershire   with lentils

Goodbye to the shooting stars too

How great to be burning

Too many years

Journals on bad love & bad weather

Tossed & Elated

Human & lazy at the end of a century

Twenty for thirty years

Then sixty for forty

Banging pots & conceptual   in search of a subject

But aren't we all

Latching on

You like Henry Cow

Me searching for gravity

Floating up

At this reading

So I knitted this

Story

Concerning the daughters of great & good intention

Born with opposable thumbs, uh-uh

Sailing through this century, ok

Honey everything   working & always

Cooking better than thinking

Practising individuation

Pushing & screaming

Multiplying bumps

In a bug

High over the River Thames

The box opens & closes the finger

The frontal lobes turn on

The Legend of, everything, everyone,

Exposed to increasingly complex displays of visual

information

Proof of reincarnation

Men generally needing more brain tissue

To make stories with

For example my flowers

Ache, The Thing & the other

Girl after girl after

Girl on fire

For socialism, for suffragettes

Streaming in flames

For rhinos & leopards

                Listing the endangered species   all four for

Three quid a month & a leaflet to save them

              Calling our silverback Norman

  Him on You Tube   Kissing his children

        Puzzled, complaining

Tweeting about the ecosystem

              We believe him

  Sent home from the hospital with no heartbeat

               & now we do this

        Out of my head—all of this—relaxing my regular

      Why I'm not Bobby Womack

Jesus I made

        Two handsome daughters

    Locked in the bedroom

Just a case of

        Pleasing yourself

  If nobody's listening   & clearly

Ambiguity's my clarity

In heaven

Because everything's possible

In a mouthful of snow

And the street, what

All shoots everywhere

Muscle relaxants   resignation

Vanishing cream, twanging

Oh! But to save this passage

Always excited vs. Always exhausted

The lips of the father

Kissing both Things

Never finished

& Impossible orbits

Push buttons for food & for love

7 mls bring down the temperature

("Eyesore")   Toothbrush floating in the toilet, Koto

Daisy

Sweet as a pastry, bright as the sun

24th December 2001

Bookshop firebombed

We do Play Doh   Operations

Carry on

This world that I hold you in

Regardless   radiant   interconnected

When the body goes wrong

Can I write it right

Wet & black books carried out in a cart

Two feet on my shoulder

Stuck here in the middle of Chinese New Year

Snow   Coats   Everything

Free   shining   dark blue   curvy

Weighing in at 108 kilos combined 3 meters 53 & rising

On the picket line again—love

In the form of an essay   with an "a"

Caught light in a bottle to recycle it

Late home from the buffalo

Moving up the anthology

But a bag's better than a bucket for vomiting

                Yellow light off the Woolwich

  Ferry

Mood swings caused by meteors

       Proved by moustache

On sabbatical from the class struggle

     For a sight of your breasts

         Only emotion endures

& inequality

          Washing the leaves of the rocket

Imploring your stars to fight it

      Great seamless moment trumpets

    A sweater knitted out of free jazz

If you get on the floor then you won't fall over

  Watching your hands   in the cold sand   delighted

       The C word's still Crap

& then humans get legs   in the painting

  All the hungry spirits, gods and buddhas who are sad

Blue green beautiful vitamins colloidal silver   shirt

                The privilege to teach poetry

But you can't teach it

        Watching the words leave my mouth

                    Too late to stop them

Useless at admonition   licked by cows   in cartoon or

    memory

            When I'm dead always socks

        The word love already

32 times in this poem

Hard not to think in terms of fuckers, though

                Circular breathing

At the grave of the catfish

   Things from the loins of the author

            The colour of a dog running

                        Red lines where a human

    was

        The cicadas in Kanazawa, almost deafening

They call me, Dad!

The swallows in Barcelona

Always arriving, always leaving

    Tigers through her

    Streets named after generals, murderers,

 dictators

Singing Happy Birthday

        In partly skies, gallopy

  Waking up with a chocolate wedged into the eighth

 vertebrate

            A drop of sweat between the book & the

  neck

Spun out of this   lullaby for pizza boys

  In the dawn   without children   giving new names to

  colours

Because I'm boring

        The bullshit drags

The baby, post-feminist

                Held together with bandages

        The father being a scribble

In the Disney book of Princesses

Inked between the legs of the witch

B being a better letter   why

Smashing & centrifugal motion

Cured by living

Honey, I will carry you home

All the way from Kingston

Past the dead doggies' graveyard

Where they lie with bad legs & whacked batteries

You screaming *CHEESE BUGGER*

Repeatedly

Unseduced

By block waves & neutrinos   moving through

The bliss-fields of concrete & language

Hiding it behind the eye

Every emotion

Incandescent

5744 minutes so far   spent on this poem

My Buddhist practice

Being useless

In a small house   barricaded in   with babies & book mould

Head chewed off of the dinosaur by bananas

Piano of the Apps,

Just before sundown

Double clutching high   non stop pine top

Intoning   in a scoob light

Hard-sounded the last nth bong of the bell

A cat comes up with a spacehat

Fixing the star with a screwdriver

Two big hits & ten licks beyond the birthday

Drunk on the contents of the lava lamp,

clean asshole poems & smiling vegetable songs

The ghost book of be-bop under the covers on the iPad

6996 words in Hairy, not

Scary   & green phosphorous   jelly

With enough light

At last in March

At 7AM

To illuminate the baby

Dragging the recorder

Sucking in the roads of SW 19

Past the bowling alley & the flyover

Sunday in the Korean quarter   to eat kim-chee

The East-Asian Jesus

Warnings on every corner

Buddha nature replaced by original sin

Proves it   but not really

The seriousness of life in a car

With a drum kit

With a father

With no sense of volume or rhythm

If you could be an insect, montage over therapy

The flowers are speaking

But I don't know what they're saying

Because I can't wait any longer

Having the great thoughts of my generation

Boat rides, how time is kept, ghosts, fluff, peaches

Afraid of the glow in the dark skeleton

We put band-aids on the purple gang   its leader called Jimi

      & your daughter the artist

Watching the water flow   uphill

          Because the government makes it so

  You accept it

In the poem about bacon, really   outraged at high table,

  Jeezus

     & the poor at the bottom

    At three, language floods in

To the world & this spinach Emily Dickinson valerian

          In the twilight at Greenwich

     Your feet on the flagstones, echoing

    If you'd only sit still

I will tell you everything, oh

Stalagmites are the ones that fall upwards

  Love all question authority pay for health insurance

    Because we   to those fuckers

  Mean nothing

Synthesizing sunlight to form others

Out of gas

On this side of the ukulele

Thing 1 & Thing 2 little homophones

One under each arm

Rolling   falling   gambolling

       This subject gladly

     Writing fast before they burn me

          Working out

How many years I spent teaching

      Just be happy

     What fuckan theory

    The kings of England, warring whoring wife-murdering

  Today is World Women's Day

Thursday March 21st International Poetry Day

Ok & hooray *for two days!*

     A whole week for potatoes

  Star cereal   & kisses   refused & accepted

       Depending on mood & appetite every day

         That food appears

Our Buddhist prayers

All life

Going in one

& out the other

Chewing Singing

Crocus   Somewhat

Among   The desires

of fathers to please mothers

The desires of mothers to please others,   rage

Abated by geranium

Poured into the broken ear

Where hills are filled with

This line from The Collected Poems of Joseph Ceravolo

Hospital clouds,

Talking to everyone

Lead you threw

The streets of London

Arrayed in loving detail

When I grow old

With no point

                              To every feeling

Lights on

                         The boss

The little button

                         Fits but tightens

The blue dress

                    The author

The daughter

                Taking apart

Flowers

                To uncover their powers

Arms stuck in

                Their head starts, their stickers

        Like a woman knocked over by pollen

I come to you

Like a lake

        Smelling of orange

Phonemes   in a suit of lights & you

Here—

Two lines at a time

without wegetables, or wi-fi

Elmer Fudd & a tonsil

Slightly inflamed

At the thought

Of friendship,   the sky the foot of everything

Not just a woman's art

Seeing, singing, sewing

Coming together in the premises

Daring to stay down

In order to say something

Without thought of confession or fame

Collaged from multiple sources

Two sperm swimming towards ink

To make love with the language

You sit at the drum kit   legs dangling   chocolate rods

High on the cymbal

Loud enough at 6AM to wake the upstairs Jamaicans

Smashy   & too small   for soldering

In Berlin   with Koalas

When I grow up   I am no longer

A sleepy tree-dwelling vegetarian

Silly boring frumpy whining & asinine   who has no stamina

Superficial, sentimental

Draggy   around the bookshop   at his best

In small cars talking

Playing & failing   over I-Spy   with my middle eye

The best reason BECAUSE I WANT TO

Stood in the middle of a cow

The heart being the seat of the intellect & emotion

In order to stay elated—

The History of Shit on an iPad   cutting off skin-tags with

scissors   when cigarettes were sexy   & beautiful coffee

How dull or exciting it all seems

With children

Living in a hole in the ground

For six years

In order to keep them

In this country

      Of sleep without women,

        Cowardly & spectacular in wet books

     Mighty Diamonds in the afternoon

     Writing   always   & standing

  My quietness has two girls in it

      "The farters of our country"

   Changing the speed of the original tape

Skyscrapers built out of bellybutton fluff

    Ready to be excited

   The father by   Hilda Morley

Who I met   once   in a chair

     All life flashing by

    Then for her, now for me

Wondrous, being now existing

      Future   Lives   All   Yours

How many feet will you   cradle

Love—

Your curve in this world

In your hands

   For good or for awful

      Velocity &

Lemons,   birds   made of half-light

Ascending   called London

Watching the radio waves

         Bend towards us   across the table   on this little

   Day every day

         Coming from & heading towards

            books, beauty

               Their achievement   & eventual   abandoning

In order to support us

Better, taller

The thwack across the back

               Signifying   the father   transcended

   At all points, not just

               One

                    Bear   in a taxi

  Mind   over carpet

                                    Swerving & burning

    Cheese string   over everything

Cleaning your cheek with a lick, yuk,

Like mum did

              Neither of us here now

                 In Toronto In 1966

       Noise the sky makes

 Triangles   impossible   sleepwrecks

 Without urine

Life is long, &

Tracking cookies

Listing stars   drooping then black murk exclamation Walt

   Living through you

Living through him

A little green

              Shadow

On the Travessera de Gracia in Barcelona

Bird on the roof

Cancels school

                       Loving you at 4:45AM so writing this

Cold ass   in poems, then

Mounting excitement

At the centre of everything, nothing

              My, your

               Disasters, happiness

                  Floods The Suburbs Revolution

Is the opium of the intellectuals

          In slippers   chickens

Leaping from eggs

Nightly, daily

   Bobbing & sleeping

 Brain cells growing

Complex sentences

Have no need to be famous

  These are the daughters who must step into the visionary

    landscape

If you love the world well enough, it will love you back

                     (The sweat pouring out)

Blok said that

      Raising your arms   above blue flowers,

                   Removing your red shirt

     Between the shoulder blades   flags   kist

Brilliant young argon upon

The wet road   running down over   the south downs I am

Caught up in you, I admit it,

     As far as the north edge of Paris

& Wild fathers,

Chalk marks between tall buildings

          Wild fathers (=wild fathers)

   Out of gas, the fruit of

The bean   or the beast

    Or the bees

      Drawn up at traffic lights,

 Covered with mirrors   Bruce Springsteen

            Forlorn but not

Forlorn Humming, the political system

Doing over beings

Over being over doing   there is

One answer, just

Sitting

When I showed you

You felt sleepy

Oh   Really   Thing 1

& I did too

The Day Lady Di Died

The day Margaret Thatcher dies

Be reborn a Buddha fireworks

When all the evil's gone

All the evils   never gone

Where the money goes

Dottr of yr father's eyes, with no room

In this place   for a man here in women

Practice   always & only of poetry politics emptiness

eternally bricklike yet

Forever setting out, never arriving

   Not building or bleeding

Bullshit, arms, abandoning, abandoned, yet

The good house Varstik! Varva! Dearest! Hamster! From

   Streatham to Morden

Written out of the canon, there were

               Three in the bed)   the song goes

& I made it

Asleep on the carpet

   Unconscious among dust mites

                  Never biting, always bitten

Holding the umbrella at the barbeque   burning the bad

   poetry

   rejecting

 the notion of salvation, all dinosaurs are good

Flying ones, the best, you don't

Follow the smell of a girl's socks

You follow the smell of a girl's feet

               Getting on by pushing

At dawn

Crossing Woolwich Ferry, Whitman saying

Resist much, Obey little,   in his hand, on pink paper

     Old enough to hold a chicken, lounging, before he

  went mad

    Calling the local cats with catnip & sandwiches

Smashing down on the burp app

 Filming the fairy lights

          Oh how I

Hate epics

Cloudless at First

Spending millions upon post-it notes & tippex   on the stairs

         Getting the first whiffs

Of mortality

  Eating the mould off goats' cheese wrapped in oak leaves

Yummy

In the distance   the faint sound of puberty

In the foreground the faint smell of poetry, money

      Bumper sticker reads HOWL if you love City Lights

Arm made of starburst

Japan, imagine that

Twice in a lifetime

    Bawling down the spillway

Naked & sweating, Hari Rama

Hari Hari

      Just a girl   made up

Or girls' things, a thumb, a faint ache beneath the right eye,

   glitter, tell me who's smashed the plates,

Lights in the smoke, dark fur past, a flower, and then another

Association, coming third in the international Beatles poetry

   competition of 1997, and then, suddenly

      A bead of sweat between the chest and the jacket

Nobody, sky, nobody

A baby

     Then eight years later

  Awake in the firmament

Made up words

   Buzzing fillings

What would Sun Ra do?

Another baby

In a man's dream

There are no novels, only poetry, beautiful cities

      Red leaf of a Japanese Maple

Brushing your eyebrow

          Strings of the ukulele

There are still so many good things in this world

      An inch deep   a mile wide

Not dead yet what

Great good fortune

     For you I'll be   por ti sere

Oh honey

When the bees have gone

     Clubbing   sleeping   shopping   into therapy

The paragraph & the sentence

In Flaubert

The father retires from the world in order to right it

Dressed like an overweight golfer from 1973, happy

Because I say so

     Often

The world is sad   because I am in it

Or because I am not

    Sat upon a badly painted horse on the south bank

Drinking the juice of an orange, cold, & the juice of a lemon

Mouth watering   like a

Dog ice kicked up the side of a hill in Mexico in a movie

     Signifying everything

Hills good   bad mountains   chalk on the neck of the ink

Two stops from tofu, she's three

    More perfect than any future

     Revolutionary letter

  Concerning roast tomatoes

We roast 'em

In handbags with lip balm berry flavor grape nails &

  swinging

Out and over the power station

Privately, without middle name or kites, my twenty-ninth

novel

Who put the pencil in your eye

Going home because I'm boring   about what

Exactly

Do you want to have an argument

Electric windows in cars   no gum   comes

From worm-juice or humans

Making a flag for make a flag day   my face

An ostrich egg in a poorly-knit nest

Upside down smiling   with the twigstand for hairway

Not off my tits, not watching Hitler docs, not allergic to

nectarines, knitting

Another fine mess

Out of all this confusion

Still life with fruit and goldfish matrimony

What is it good for?

Absolutely

There's a shadow hanging over me

It is the concept of self, clearly

Similar to a zither

Buttering pancakes with the blunt bit of the knife

Growing hair on the side of the head

Light from the crystal fills the room

We step on it   nature   work

Contains foul language

On the edge of the Thames, at Putney

Wrists covered with monster munch dust

On the monorail through the financial zone, explicit

language about red deer

Rearranging the molecules in front of your face

Does books include The Tim Atkins Annual

And you are

Just a girl in sandals

Making enquiries about samphire

Practicing to be a woman

Asking the Oulipo for advice   about ants

Is the bible fiction, daddy, or

Science Fiction, eating a banana

From each

According to his ability

To each according to her need

Having brownouts, kids

In McD's having a poo, babe

Being racist to green M&Ms, oh, throwing them

Forget it, at the

Mixed girl & chips, or

Kentucky Fried Children, every year

I cannot feel whole when so knowingly forgetting

The death of 50 billion chicken, postmodern American

Poetry, nerve damage, Van Morrison

Against this

What does it mean to be human? The limits of my language,

looking

at a fish

In peace, finally,

The New Wave of British Heavy Pedantry, ducks on the

millpond

Alive, finally

Wearing the products of sweatshops

                  T-shirt says DUDES   stretching it

  How did your ass end up on the cactus

Exactly, in the action replay

I would kiss you the same, steeply, blown off

The top of the Malvern Hills

          Three peaches in a dish, and a green light over

  what

          I thought were called mumps

In the poem

Children dance to the static, we are

          The Atkins family

It says in the poem   tiny & exotic   we get

     7 out of 10 for language

                    8 instances of the word fuck in a poem

  About & for children, really

          In a past life, a bagel

        All you could see were the coats moving

The reports always said

Could do better

Food, the family unit, mood

The great poets of the UK, O, Jeff!

Tapping the hamster app at 6AM then

Plane crashes into the beats   '

The primary cause of global warming, I am

Discussing guns   at the barbeque   with the new dads

Yeah they say yeah   fascinated & appalling

Using a magnifying glass

To watch shadows   passing over

Professional spiders

Thistember

10 feet up in the oak   with a saw   for

To stop the baby   crying   for

To rescue the daughter

The books on my shelf, Anselm Hollo, Hilda

Morley

Beauty and the labour of mourning

94

Heat builds in the finger, the finger fingers

      A lonely beast the dell Vikings, the iodines, peels a

  sticker

The birds eat the plants, the plants eat the cats, the cats eat

  the humans

  Extract them with an artist's brush

Canned air, hair stylistics

                Watch the poets dying

Welcome to my beard, it is

     A miserable stick up   to a lily

Measured by beard-weight

   If our mother of monster say

     PLAY! PLAY! then   we   will   play

    SORE NANOHANA!   Hurry! Rape blossoms! Hurry!

   Naughty Manifesto of Futurist Kids, Jazz of the Civil War

     Smashed into the carpet

Five-year-olds can drive, see

Removing your lunch from your knee, the

Cat flap

Too small

To leap through

Saving up to pay

The entry fee to enter the poetry competition

For here are the new forms

Manifestos grant applications   inflatables

Concerning the world

Book launch   Fuck them   With bongos

What do you do if your hamster needs more room

What do you do in Cordoba with your vegetarianism

Tidy your work space

Or write a polemic

We do not spend Sunday in the ball pool

We spend it in a warehouse with a teenager dressed as a tiger

then

Take a pin to your splinter

Voice missing because

You threw it into the sky

Just a piece of seaweed at the recital

With dookey hair neons & hoop earrings

Abstractly living lullabies

Now embroider words

Keep our tiny owls

And leak light

Where she is clumsy in parts

And hold her

In our normal condition

Without agitation

Boom, boom, boom

Wherever you are

Life   getting in the way   occasionally

A palpitation like an envelope forecasting doom

That cannot undo the glue

I have for you   (Tim)

Free and red in your

Star, centrifugal

Nature also seemed

Shining with tea

Can in Elf-light

Rearranges reckless sorrow

Parallels in economic russet   herald the Mongolian

green algae

We are not looking for a master   in cosmic Elk Grass

We are looking for the marbles

Through which to view   A little blinking   light sandwich, or

Satellite attachment, we all

Sigh at least sometimes

As surprise is tragic and satisfies our human feelings

For a period of unbelief

Bending in retreat   eroded by solar wind

In an imaginary field

Remembering the teeth of your can

Travels down your leg   narrative

A substitute for emotion

Little daughters

In the middle of the night

50 photos cost nothing

The stars are raindrops searching for a place to fall

Eroded by solar wind, my

Own Face

Eroded by solar wind, by

Rain on the lips

Until there is none poppy

Six petals gone

Days growing darker

Before they had a chance to grow light

The Conservative tax on sunshine

After too much of it under the previous administration

All the same, there is

War all the time

"In the practice of Zen"   all is War is Over, if

Well, you decide

Wife happy sleeping

Children happy   Sunday afternoon

Emptiness

Almost touching

Father's Day

The bodhisattva Manjushri

Of wisdom and intellect—

        almost touching

  Ko Un said

Eat your food.

When you've eaten, go shit

Oh

Doing it

Wrong

      But, with

  Compassion and full attention

        A plane coming out of the clouds

  Daddy   daddy

  Sweeping rice krispies into a pink plastic dustpan, asking

        Did you drop them or throw them?

Suddenly interested in the ceiling

    One gray hair

  Arriving, hello

Upon the left eyebrow

Moving back to read the screen   forward to type

Blue & pink   ink leaks on sheets   getting out of bed

On the wrong side

On the other

By popcorn light

Wedding band of kryptonite, yet

Because Superman's   not fucked

In the novel, we all are

Red and orange that keeps beeping,

My wildebeast

With a bagel of quietus / and bright limits

Stitches that itches

Sick with Freddie Mercury

Poisoning

By the edge of the municipal pool, paddling   excited (1)

Or (2) freezing

Dragging the dead father

Then dropping

The head stream

The cactus gas

With no bed

No Pleiades

In the psychometric test

Anger on canals   beside myself   Outside gated

   developments

    Drinking the lights

        Living the life

All life therein   emails

       Thing 1 sleeping

Thing 2 sleeping   Father

Typing

Miss Dior in duty free shops

All that's left of my mother, my mother

        A TV shark's not a babysitter

   God is—Dad—if

           Licking the mixture, I will

        Catch you when you fall

In a cathedral car

Swimming from school to school

Drying out by fluorescent light

—Then the needle goes in—

And you flip

—Oh

Enough to wipe out a year's worth of writing

     Drinking cocktails of zinc & aluminium

        So the craft doesn't land on the cervix,

 everywhere

  Bad lawyers, bad

Doctors, inoculations against traffic, nature, compassion

    & against them

    A skin brush & a room

In a cloud of red powder   the homeopathic novel   honey

    Party for your right to fight

But what or who   the bad guys do

   The daughter, the

Daughter

Their future becomes

Counter revolutionary,   Date rape at readings

The Chinese rolling into Tibet & then over it

Pu Ling-en   still appalled by his shit

                  as   you bleep me with gadgets

   the hamburger store T-shirt says

Our food shits on your food / the hamburger store T-shirt says

To vegetarians

All carnivores are capitalists, ignorance =

A ham sandwich

                  Dropped off the monkey bars

Telling the truth about drugs to your children   in popular

   song

Every time there's a knock on the door we drop to the floor

                  Dumpster diving

                  MY! POETICS!

   "Just" "saying"

Just saying

These are the daughters who must step out of the visionary

104

landscape

Counting their teeth

Deciding their worth

The tiger in the drawing of the tiger with flowers

Impossible   because   of the mother all of us

Signed up to serve

The rich

Chased by big dogs with bumblebees in their mouths

   spitting them out at your arse

Welcome to nihilism

You fail the nationality test

   Cheese is not Lego, and Lego is not cheese

One thing a father can learn from a daughter—amazement

Coming second   after Russell Atkins

            Then the Needle Goes In

                    My daughter after

What is left? What is gone?

         Dreaming of death, a

New & selected

Fallen on by hormone

First sniff of the end of it

The cradle rocks above an abyss, I am

Still "in love" with poetry, I feel

Everything and see nothing

On a stairway to heaven, a

    Seasonal Affective Disorder   in everything   on a highway

    to hell, &

all cats

Are beautiful tattoos   beneath

Fallen arches   an optician's neither

an artist nor terrorist

    Scraping ice off the baby   after sex

2005, 2006

       How do you *turn* a book *on*? Or *turn* on a book?

In all things   big clouds

    At the pop tart eating competition, is this

A leg to be climbed in

          Going to school   dress-as-a-book-character day

in school uniform

Dressed as Mr Forgetful

Laughing till asses get slapped   still   not buying a cat

No more treats, no more anything, till you come back from

Iceland

In a car on a road   in the dark

sick of everything   love governments

your new spaghetti gloves   keep the floor warm not

fingers   tread them in

sick of money   sick of dusk   sick of men & of women, sick

of borders & customers

Pigs in dungarees & ducks in boots   chickens that sing

We still eat 'em

Cheating at everything

in order to win food, feelings, for

This is my schtic

Going over Niagra in a barrel

Kissing in beds

Is like nobody going to the reading,

or

Just a glorified licking

When the electrics

        I can see your bones

  & don't need a manifesto around "tenderness"   it just is

        Coated in breadcrumbs, this print-on-

demand

   Sleeplessness, dominos, rocksteady, hot body, foot says

  I love you   rushing through space   towards my face   &

  then smashing in

   The library cuts

Candy makes me

Ouchy

      We do not talk about beheadings (yet)

We talk about what we did in the neck & the spots

         & the cuts

& the cuts

On commons, roads, car seats, parks, donut shops, arks

You will have

108

The blood & the milk & the dance & the babies

     & us men

  With this void & these daughters against everything   it

feels a little

squeaks if not oiled

    Here through a hole in your earlobe

A girl considering vegetarianism through the lens of Beyoncé

Because a girl is a machine made of words

               & only within this system does

  each particle attain

    A joke involving eyeballs

   Because one leg = flapping   & 3 says

  LEAVE ME ALONE

With the coati mundi & the word search & the mobile phones

        Where will you be, my little

  daughters

When I am old and alone

    I shall wear my hair   instead of Emily

      For what does it feel to be loved in this

world

                                        When

you are old and alone

        Carp should not be this big

    3 peas mean I can get down

                        Helpful with

anything dangerous

        The whole of October   I will never be your ruler

For obvious reasons

 Insisting upon the name   Dr Funkenstein

   All of the fathers   as tiny as sperm   at the end   of a

   bed

        Weighing the beauty of daughters

Against the hell of all else

                    But it *was* good

To visit capitals

    And to leave them it was good

                        to see your crayons

In a fine frenzy, rolling

110

Oh, good, daddy, bad

Cop   until sundown   she places an X

Where the bad mothers are   believed to be

good

Penguins, birds, vultures

Fathers all sitting   for peace   in the dark

As unpopular as love is, as socialism, the father is

Shining the shoes, he is

Invisible, inviolable, uncomfortable

For these are the South London boroughs & we owls

have been driven out of the bohemian quarters to inhabit

them

In our nests, in our knees, with our books & CDs

& always the cuts

& these poems

Always   against   them,

Stars   rules   lists

Flying kids, magic, chips, dirt in a box, string of lights,

checklists

Checking out, checking off

                    All the reasons the government hates us

    Beings, artists, tiny resistors, mixed somethings, second

    sex, singers, sock losers, sorbet makers, pill poppers,

    almost pure to the point of pointlessness

Frying slices of Sun Ra in a pan

        The day already done

                     Like a life in a line

In order to what   graduate   aged five-and-three-quarters

    I told you it was

The curriculum of being human

    When really it was just shit

All the time

      I love you , just because

Fathers want to say it

& be beings who say it

         Married to concrete, in this corner, though

Always hoping for global warming   again & again & again

            The thing that I got is the thing that

you want like a sandwich

& then all human history

You made this, thus

            You do not have diplomatic immunity

aged 13, this

        Fucking spring, fucking summer, fucking autumn,

    fucking winter, again & again & again

            the double dream of thing,   the

Ren & the bubs

It falling on all humankind, not

The holocaust, but a holocaust, one

        Fast on the heels of

Another

                    Because all anyone wants is to be

    famous or anonymous

On a bench   with a sandwich

        & 20 teeth in the mouth

                    Talking about   Barbie's arm,

    magical

Fairy girls in the costumes of prostitutes

                        Coming back from a holiday

Daddy, where's my present?

              I'm your present!

What?

          The only way to tell the season in this country is

  the length of your socks

               Beans do not inspire a girl

               Nor do grains or greens

                       Noseless people

In felt tip on your feet

       Climb the leg, the leg

  That won't stop   calling, exploring

              needing, feeding

              confiding, all these things

A daddy does not get

About daughters—

About 50 years, maybe, &

The future of Fascism

I love you from all mothers, the father

Dieing daily for the lack of that, the

Sleep deprived

Parents, the children

Alive for less than a thousand months

    Jumping up and down

          In the exhibit about insects

        Squashing them, screaming

  I can see their brains! On the floor! Look!

         Still moving!

Praying to Jah you grow out of it

            The way to bring up a human being

Not revenge but compassion, the assholes

Around us, all

Asshole & dreaming

           A natural reaction

in both policy & poems, Koto,   only in those who lack

Imagination

       The key question being how to both love &

Overcome them

     When we would rather be swimming (shouting) or

sewing

     Cutting the ghosts out of notebooks   & spinning

them from strings off the ceiling

   Saying hello to the new vegetables

Increasing our brand recognition

            Corn, always

 Looking good in your pigtails

The taxi, the daddy

       Saying your names

  To my body   in places to keep it

From drowning

      How much of the heat of the sun does one need

To escape from IKEA?

How many needles to get through Cecil Taylor?

      Enough

Teeth moving around the face, sleep failing, you

  Only need me when you want something, sedatives,

strawberries

Summer

Just a bubble in a puddle

Sweating in a train full of tories

The day after the election, the living dead

All of us

Sold, sold out, selling

The dinosaur on the cake climbing the

skyscraper   to destroy us

With its legs, no, fuck it, and storming off

Because fierce is as fierce does, just

The fragments of a human

Sneezing into Lego

The tattoo just a black smudge

Beard, glasses & earring

The Selected Tom

With one unpublished poem

We are here to ____ each other, after all

The invisible deficit

In the corner of the room

Humming

Just a girl, wrapped

in a blanket

A caterpillar covered in hydrogen

peroxide

Looks for her father

A peony's head touches the window, it was sunny, now it's

dark, I'm bored

And sad about London   the planes making clouds

Over privatized parks, crumbling hospitals, unoccupied

second homes

Hammering,   to fix it

Tears squirt from the face

We film it

On the demo again

Writing poems, making linocuts

We pray to Duke Ellington

A toothache

For poetry = an evolutionary playlist

a) Floating bear

In the Thames

Clouds look good   from above b) we all look

good

The Atkins Family

Upon Christmas cards   in the same costume,

The same sentiments for the

same old worlds

For how long can you keep your head under water

In books, in New Malden

INS &   ERS

Shitting, shining

dropping

living

letters

Fading, polyester,   sincerely, finally

Cheating at snakes & ladders

to beat a panda

Biting down on the daddy   to keep him from drowning

                    You get a sticker for that

Come down here right now

  & get your snot off the ceiling

On Fathers < On Daughtyrs
By Tim Atkins

First published in this edition by Boiler House Press 2017
Part of UEA Publishing Project
All rights reserved
© Tim Atkins 2017

The right of Tim Atkins to be identified as the author of this work
has been asserted in accordance with the with the Copyright,
Design & Patents Act, 1988.

Design and typesetting by Emily Benton
emilybentonbookdesigner.co.uk
Typeset in Arnhem
Printed by Imprint Digital, UK
Distributed by NBN International

ISBN 978-1-911343-20-2